DISCOVER PHYSICAL SCIENCE

DISCOVER MOTION

by Tammy Enz

PEBBLE
a capstone imprint

Pebble Emerge is published by Pebble, an imprint of Capstone.
1710 Roe Crest Drive, North Mankato, Minnesota 56003
www.capstonepub.com

Library of Congress Cataloging-in-Publication Data is available
Names: Enz, Tammy, author.
Title: Discover motion / by Tammy Enz.
Description: North Mankato, MN : Pebble, [2021] | Series: Discover physical science |
    Includes index. | Audience: Ages 5-7 | Summary: "Take a look out the window.
    What do you see? People, cars, bikes, birds, and more are all on the move. With
    this basic introduction to motion, young readers will discover the three laws of
    motion, what they mean, and how they affect our lives every day"—Provided
    by publisher.
Identifiers: LCCN 2020001053 (print) | LCCN 2020001054 (ebook) |
    ISBN 9781977124432 (hardcover) | ISBN 9781977126290 (paperback) |
    ISBN 9781977124869 (eBook PDF)
Subjects: LCSH: Motion—Juvenile literature.
Classification: LCC QC127.4 .E59 2021 (print) | LCC QC127.4 (ebook) |
    DDC 531/.11—dc23
LC record available at https://lccn.loc.gov/2020001053
LC ebook record available at https://lccn.loc.gov/2020001054

Summary: Describes the key concepts behind motion and how they work
in our world.

Image Credits
Capstone Studio: Karon Dubke, 21; iStockphoto: SDI Productions, 19; Newscom:
Blend Images/Roberto Westbrook, 9; Shutterstock: 3Dsculptor, 18, Air Images,
5, akihirohatako, 14, Doug Lemke, Cover, Georgios Kollidas, 7, Kang Sunghee, 17,
mTaira, 15, Oleg Mikhaylov, 6, SmartPhotoLab, 13, Stingray Pro, 11

Design Elements
Capstone; Shutterstock: Immersion Imagery

Editorial Credits
Editor: Aaron Sautter; Designer: Hilary Wacholz; Media Researcher:
Jo Miller; Production Specialist: Spencer Rosio; Set Stylist: Marcy Morin

All internet sites appearing in back matter were available and accurate when this
book was sent to press.

Printed and bound in China.
PO3322

Table of Contents

Words in **bold** are in the glossary.

WHAT IS MOTION?

Pedal your bike. Run across the park. What are you doing? You are moving!

When things move, they have **motion**. Motion is a big part of our lives. Look all around you. Things are always on the move!

THE LAWS OF MOTION

Have you ever thrown or bounced a rubber ball? It bounces off the walls and floor. You never know where it will go. But wait. There is a way you can know!

Sir Isaac Newton was a scientist in the 1600s. He discovered the three **laws of motion**. Things that move follow these laws. They tell us exactly how something moves.

Sir Isaac Newton

THE FIRST LAW OF MOTION

Think about a toy truck sitting on the floor. Is it moving? No. But it still follows Newton's first law of motion. It says that things that aren't moving will stay still.

The truck only moves if a **force** acts on it. If you push the truck, you use a force. If you pull it with a string, that is also a force. If the wind blows the truck, that's a force too.

The first law of motion has a second part. It says if something is moving, it keeps moving. It doesn't stop or change direction. It keeps going unless a force acts on it.

Give the toy truck a push on a rug. It slows down and stops. What stops it? The wheels rub on the rug. This creates **friction**. This force slows the truck until it stops.

11

THE SECOND LAW OF MOTION

Push a toy car as hard as you can. What happens? It moves pretty far, right? But what if you tried to push a real car as hard as you can? It might not move at all.

Newton's second law of motion says an equal force moves things differently. The toy car is light. A push moves it easily. A real car is heavy. The same push won't move it.

There is another part to the second law of motion. It says bigger forces move things faster and farther. Smaller forces move things only a little.

Swing a bat and hit a baseball really hard. What happens? It flies fast and far. Now give the ball a small tap. The ball moves slowly. It goes only a short distance.

THE THIRD LAW OF MOTION

Newton's third law of motion is important. It says forces are **equal** and **opposite**. What does that mean?

When you sit in a chair, you push down on it. But it pushes up on you too. How do you know? The chair holds you up. You and the chair both push with the same force.

Think about a rocket flying into space. Gases from burning **fuel** push on the rocket. The rocket also pushes on the gases. The opposite forces help the rocket fly!

Clap your hands. You can feel the third law at work. Your hands hit with the same force. Let's all clap our hands for motion! Motion helps us go places and do fun things.

MOTION FLICK TEST

Supplies:

3 cardboard food boxes, different sizes

smooth floor or table

Directions:

1. Set the boxes on the floor or table.

2. Line them up from smallest and lightest
   to biggest and heaviest.

3. Start with the lightest box. Flick it with
   your finger. See how far it moves.

4. Now flick each of the other boxes. Which box moved the most? Which law of motion explains this?

Glossary

equal (EE-kwul)—the same as something else in size or amount

force (FORS)—something that pushes or pulls

friction (FRIK-shuhn)—a force produced when objects rub together, causing them to slow down

fuel (FYOOL)—anything that can be burned to give off energy

laws of motion (LAWZ uhv MOH-shuhn)—the three rules in science that describe how and why objects move

motion (MOH-shuhn)—moving or being moved

opposite (OP-uh-zit)—as different as possible

Read More

James, Emily. *The Simple Science of Motion*. North Mankato, MN: Capstone, 2018.

Peterson, Megan Cooley. *Motion*. North Mankato, MN: Pebble, 2020.

Rivera, Andrea. *Motion*. Minneapolis: ABDO Zoom, 2018.

Internet Sites

Newton's Three Laws of Motion
https://thekidshouldseethis.com/post/newtons-three-laws-of-motion-royal-observatory-greenwich

Physics for Kids: Laws of Motion
https://www.ducksters.com/science/laws_of_motion.php

Index